MOVEMENTS IN M

SURREA

MOVEMENTS IN MODERN ART

Peter de Francia: IMPRESSIONISM

Denis Mathews: FAUVISM

Edith Hoffmann: EXPRESSIONISM

Alfred Schmeller: CUBISM
(Translated by Hilde Spiel)

Alfred Schmeller: SURREALISM
(Translated by Hilde Spiel)

Frederick Gore: ABSTRACT ART

ALFRED SCHMELLER

SURREALISM

WITH 24 ILLUSTRATIONS

CROWN PUBLISHERS, INC.

NEW YORK

Translated by Hilde Spiel

Reproduction Rights: S.P.A.D.E.M., Paris, and Cosmopress, Geneva
Printed in Austria
by Brüder Rosenbaum, Vienna

SURREALISM

Surrealism is a term often wrongly used to circumscribe the whole of modern painting. It would be hardly less erroneous, however, to confine it to paintings of the Surrealist school without bearing in mind that its aims have found a purer and clearer expression in poetry, and possibly even in films.

For the Surrealist programme was not concerned merely with aesthetics. It was a comprehensive attempt to create a new attitude towards life, a new pattern of existence, a corrected vision of the world, which manifested itself mainly in writing. Within the Surrealist trend or movement, painting in fact played a solitary and even a minor part. The reason for this is that Surrealism was essentially a literary movement, and, at bottom, not even wholly that. It was a revolutionary event in the ideological history of our century which used the media of literature, philosophy and journalism, and every kind of public expression, including painting, but including also graphic art, photography, the cinema. Surrealist painting, therefore, took a comparatively modest place. Indeed, it won esteem merely on the strength of a few artists of genius, not because it created its own vision or added substantially to the programme evolved by the movement as a whole. Its impulse sprang from writing, from the cerebrations of others than painters. This introduction, therefore, must deal with the phenomenon of Surrealism as a whole, and use its painting by way of illustration.

Surrealism differs fundamentally from all other artistic movements of our time in that it springs from a much wider context and stakes an all-embracing claim. Expressionist painting developed quite apart from literary Expressionism in some isolated groups of painters ("Der blaue Reiter", "Die Brücke") and in individual artists. Cubism was predominantly and intrinsically a school of painting which initiated, or was accompanied by, parallel trends in prose, poetry, and architecture. Exponents of Surrealism, however, far more than those of Expressionism, claimed for themselves a total transformation of life. As distinct from Impressionists, Fauves, and abstract artists, they propounded a Surrealist "way of existence". From this it may be seen that, loudly proclaimed though it has been, Surrealism has dwelt merely on the fringe of modern art. Its attitude towards life, however, was clearly foreshadowed in earlier centuries.

Today, Surrealism must be judged in relation to its time. It is unthinkable without war. Indeed, it first arose as a reaction to the futility of the First World War. In 1916 a few poets, painters, and composers exiled in Zurich had founded the Cabaret Voltaire and issued a number of publications under the title of Dada — the rocking horse. The word sounds like a baby's babbling. "We derided simply everything, nothing was sacred to us, we spat on it all: that was Dada. It was neither Mysticism nor Communism nor Anarchism. All these 'isms' had some sort of a programme. We, however, were purely, completely Nihilist, and our symbol was the null and void, the vacuum, the hole." Thus the painter George Grosz, who belonged to the Berlin Dada group.

Similar publications appeared in Paris where young artists and writers had declared themselves to be "moderns" utterly opposed to any kind of tradition, defining their programme as modernness as such, the new spirit, the poetical experiment at any price, a sort of literary *va banque*, the eternal surprise. Their driving force was the poet Guillaume Apollinaire, who in 1917, in one of his letters, coined the term "Surrealism". Among the initiators of Dadaism was Tristan Tzara who later fell out wth André Breton, the initiator of Surrealism. Dadaism was a revolt, a rebellion against war. It proclaimed total nonsensicality as a weapon against the various ways in which war was supposed to make sense, for Dadaists considered war to be nonsense *per se*. It proclaimed the total destruction of all values which until then had seemed sacred, it ridiculed patriotism, honour, religion, ambition, human greatness, and every kind of ideal, and tore the masks from all false gods. In this Dadaism was akin to Surrealism, its offspring. The leading Surrealists, Aragon, Breton, Eluard and Péret had been the founders of the French group of Dadaists.

From this climate Surrealism was born. Everywhere the profound psychological depression left behind, in the sensitive minds of artists, by war and mass sacrifice in the name of mankind's most sacred possessions, found release. In Paris the ground was prepared by innovators, revolutionary minds thirsting for new ways of expression. Dadaism kindled a spark in all the major cities of Europe; the air was filled with a mixture of defeatism, a sell-out of reason, a renunciation of logical behaviour, which was blamed for the war and its aftermath of chaos and ruin. Thus a movement and a method were born, and an idea gained ground.

"I announce to the world a trifle of tremendous importance: a new vice has come into the world, one more virtue has been given to man — Surrealism, son of bright enthusiasm and of darkness. Walk up, walk up: here you'll find the most wonderful snapshots!" These words from Aragon's "Le Paysan de Paris". (1924) uttered in the manner of a tout on the fair-ground, are the beginning of Surrealist literature. It was the genius of André Breton who divined and theoretically defined this fresh method, this new idea. In contrast to its forerunners it was no longer purely destructive and anarchist, but became increasingly conscious of its means. It can be said that there was "method in this madness". Amidst a group of young *literati*, Breton discovered this point of departure, and went on to propagate Surrealism not as an aesthetic movement, but as an instrument of conception and cognition.

As far as it developed in Paris, where it constituted one of the sharpest emanations of French thinking between the wars, the Surrealist movement extended between the two crucial dates of 1918 and 1939. It had its preparatory period, its heroic period from 1923 until 1925, its critical phase between 1925 and 1930, and its autonomous phase thereafter until 1939. The group became immensely active. Publications, handbills, pamphlets, following each other in quick succession, inundated the whole of Paris. The manifestoes were an attempt at clarification of aims and intentions. Seldom has there been a group of *literati* who devoted so much thought and theoretical speculation to their own creative methods. There was an avalanche of protests; the Pope was attacked, and so was Paul Claudel; trials were staged in defence of freedom of thought; scandal after scandal was provoked; radical slogans were coined against family life, the state, religion; self-destruction was encouraged in statements and debates. There were expulsions, splits. A number of the spokesmen went over to Communism and remain there still. Political problems gave rise to new crises. There was a Bureau for Surrealist Research. Exhibitions were organized — in 1938 fourteen countries took part.

Up to 1930 paintings by Picasso were reproduced in Surrealist publications without being considered specifically Surrealist. Beside him, there were connected with the movement Giorgio de Chirico who during the First World War had called his painting *pittura metafisica*, Joan Miró, André Masson and, above all, Max Ernst, whose work probably came nearest to Surrealism as visualized by the Surrealists themselves. A canvas by Max Ernst "The Rendez-vous of Friends" (1922) shows amongst others Jean Arp, de Chirico, Ernst, but also Raphael. After 1930 Salvador Dali joined the group, and from 1934 onwards it comprised, among artists, Ernst, Dali, Arp, Tanguy, de Chirico, the sculptor Giacometti, and the painters Magritte, Brauner, Miró, and Man Ray.

During the Second World War the Surrealists dispersed. Péret went to Mexico, Breton and others to various American countries. Thus Surrealism spread also to the New World. When Breton returned to France in 1946, he was honoured as one of the great representatives of French cultural life. After the Second World War Surrealism continued to widen its circles, reaching out to nearly every country of the free world. The Venice Biennale of 1954 gave proof of the existence of Surrealist painters in Greece and Guatemala, in Austria and Canada, in Belgium and Brazil.

Today the turbulent dissipations of early Surrealism are viewed with tolerance. The work of Breton and Eluard, Aragon and Péret has been accepted within the realm of French literature. Eluard, Aragon and others, incidentally, were members of the Résistance.

In his "Manifesto of Surrealism" (1924) Breton was able to formulate: "Surrealism is sheer psychological automatism, by means of which it is intended to express verbally, in writing, or in some other way, the

8

actual function of thinking. Dictation of thinking, without any control exercised by reason, outside any aesthetic or moral prejudice."

The stream of consciousness emerges in *écriture automatique*, automatic writing, in fantasies and states of hallucination, in accounts of dreams, in absurd games. Man tries to shake off his tunnelling and constructing intellect which runs in grooves, along well-tried tracks, and is drilled to think in fixed categories; and simply records, copies, or portrays. Man under automatic dictation is inwardly wide awake; he listens to his inner self and adapts himself to it, more a fisherman casting his net than a trapper setting his trap. This is his state of inspiration. Logic is eliminated, the process by which universal conclusions are obtained is reversed, and the supreme authority of the causative system is abolished. By means of the very logic which such a view of life rejects, it is not difficult to see how a connection was established between Surrealist method and the anti-Christian, Communist view of history and politics.

Surrealism, as will be seen, is first of all discovery, the opening-up of new material worlds, the search for the unconscious. Over and over again Surrealists have paid homage to Freud and referred to him at every stage; some of them even began as psychiatrists.

One of the realms of experience claimed by Surrealists is therefore found in dream, dream with its absurd encounters and transformations, its paradoxical combinations. Dream is seen as a wholly equal partner to wakefulness. Indeed, increased attention is paid to the existence of man while dreaming; waking thought is relegated to a secondary position; and the sum of moments experienced in dream taken for true reality on a par with moments experienced in waking.

Here it should be pointed out that many Surrealist paintings strongly resemble dreams or rather dream situations. Thus the "landscapes of the soul" by Max Ernst, Dali, or Tanguy, with their inner worlds of glassy rigidity, their precious density, their diamond hardness, their cold gem-like strangeness. Sharply lit, their contours stand out with crystal clarity; they give an impression of being heightened dream images.

9

Surrealism relies throughout on realistic means. These painters paint faithfully, imitatively, true to their subject. Everything is recognisable in their pictures, all objects can be named. Yet these well-known objects are used in a fantastic manner, they are freely linked in a way unheard-of in our conscious, wakeful, purposeful reality. This hidden dimension the term Sur-realism — Super-realism — tries to convey.

This approach to painting adheres at least partly to traditional conceptions, refrains from upsetting visual practices which have been in use for centuries, and thus facilitates understanding. To some extent Surrealist paintings are reflections, but reflections of an underlying world which, in some mysterious way, has been broken up into fragments, leaving cracks and fractured lines to hint at new associations. But these fragments at least have remained large enough for us to recognise objects, trees, human beings, or rocks. In Cubism, especially in its early phase, the fragments to which reality was reduced were so small, so minutely tessellated, that reality seemed to be lost altogether. Some Surrealist pictures, on the other hand, recall a Chinese puzzle.

In describing its peculiar realms, in translating hallucinations or the shadowy experience of a dream into the terms of a hard world of objects, Surrealist painting remains in the tradition of what, since the Renaissance, has been regarded as realist art. Where it differs from this is in the moonlight quality of the pictures, in their harsh midnight sun, their desert light, their alienation. All this should not be confused with Romanticism. How vastly different is the Romantic approach with its sentimental, humanizing tendencies, its *Schwärmerei*, its melting-away in emotion, its transformation of the world through feeling, its climate of boundlessness and frayed edges! In Surrealism limits are drawn everywhere, clear cuts are made, all is divided up, outlined, newly linked; one border only is deliberately not recognized: the border between dream and wakefulness.

Some of these paintings show the importance of total war as a begetter of this mood, the fiery furnace in which all things are hardened and tempered in rainbow colours as on a steely surface. Dreamland, after all, corresponds closely to the alien experience of war, to no-man's-land, the desolate zone of annihilation. Some pictures seem as if taken after a bombardment; they have a strange sharpness. Dust which has settled over the destruction alters the plastic dimension of objects. The customary inter-relation of objects is suspended. Pictures look like still-lifes arranged by a demolition squad. Total alienation has been achieved.

These pictures show landscapes empty like a stage, consisting of flat areas in which objects are presented in stark relief. Frequently the edges are blocked up by mountain scenery, by bizarre rocks. On this stage, objects and human beings are arranged haphazard. Watches have become soft as butter, they begin to melt and drip, they resemble poached eggs. Human shapes are presented like chests with many drawers. There are pictures of jungles, and dead cities. The entire meticulous technique of miniature painting, the delicate mechanics of exact reproduction are placed at the service of a displaced, shifted, borderline frame of mind. Clocks show the wrong time.

Space, too, is wrecked by the Surrealists as they break categorically with the common concept of dimensions. Anywhere an abyss may open, a tomb may gape. The four walls of a room have become permeable. You may look or glide through a floor, you may filter through a ceiling. Certainly this is a compact and tangibly realistic world, but upon closer inspection it appears to have been transformed with the help of a new dimension. Shape, body, even the details of objects have remained the same, but a new dimension of mutual permeability and penetration has been added. As a theme of Surrealist painting, this permeability alternates with typical "landscapes of the soul" — wide expanses of sand or salt desert on which objects or occurrences are scattered at random. Such a desert is the favourite background of Salvador Dali's paintings, as may be seen from Plates 7 and 8 in this volume.

Dream is a means of mastering alienation, of fixing it, and of retaining the characteristics of the uncanny, the singular, the incomprehensible, and the irrational. As laid down by Breton: "Surrealism is based on belief in the importance of certain forms of association hitherto neglected, in the omnipotence of dream, in the purposeless game of thinking. It aims at the final annihilation of all other psychological mechanisms, and at taking their place in solving the foremost problems of life."

The importance of certain forms of association is also interpreted by the "Surrealist object" — objects found and picked up at random, to be combined in still-lifes. They play an important part as a sort of "Surrealist sculpture". Any object taken from its original surroundings, torn from its context, or used in a new and unknown way, will fit the picture. (Anyone who has visited a painter's studio will have seen odd discoveries hanging on the walls or lying about — roots, old toys, bottles — capable of stimulating the imagination, of acting as thought fetishes, as the mandrake in black magic.) They were once described by de Chirico: "Furniture taken from its habitual place acquires a particular, strong expressiveness — for instance, when seen in the street, during a removal. A strange and inaccessible happiness seems to emanate from these blessed, unknown little islands. They are a sanctuary. Imagine an arm-chair, a divan, chairs placed in a group in some deserted spot of Greece, or in the American prairie. Conversely, nature surrounding them shows a face which we have never seen before. For some time I have been obsessed by the impression made by furniture outside a house. In several paintings I have tried to express this feeling. I find all these emotional undercurrents echoed in a curious painting by Cocteau: A landscape, with two walls and a chair. It was the opposite of a ruin; these were bits of a future palace . . ." Surrealists are for ever quoting from the "Chants of Maldoror" by the "Comte de Lautréamont" (Isidore Ducasse, 1846—1870), one of their forefathers and models, rediscovered by them and never since abandoned, especially his formula: "Beauty: the possibility of a sewing machine and an umbrella meeting on the dissecting table."

This is a discovery which may be made on the ticker tape of psychological automatism. Surrealist form consists in a similar apposition. In paintings the objects are spread out, in poetry they are strung together without punctuation, equipoised. In a litany the conscious region of the mind is kept occupied and thereby put out of action, so that the unconscious may function all the more freely. Automatism, uninterrupted goings-on, create an atmosphere in which Surrealists can meditate. There are no developments, everything proceeds simultaneously; the even trot, the traces of objects on the plain; intoxication through monotony; the preference for rain; the absence of gradients, of gradation, of climax; the effacement of classic composition. A climate of primeval myths: inaudibly, there is music in all things. The most heterogeneous impressions suddenly unite in a melody, turn into a poem.

Man proposes *and* disposes, says Breton. It is up to him wholly to belong to himself, that is, to keep the daily more threatening fetters of his desire in a constant state of anarchy. Poetry teaches him how to achieve this. "It is a question of returning to the sources of poetic imagination and, what is far more difficult, of staying there." Surrealism thus considers poetry to be a method of cognition, by which man may discover the unrevealed regions of his mind. Surrealists have a more comprehensive conception of man than could formerly be gained by logical reasoning. They recognize motives, appetites, desires, and do not overlook the psychological subsoil of man which, if suppressed, becomes overpowering. In the last resort, all the catastrophic events of our time were due to the fact that the lower reaches of man's soul, having been neglected, denied, and rendered inaudible by numerous moral and conventional considerations, end up by exercising overweening power.

Surrealism is an instrument enabling us to climb into the inner region and to light up the power reservoir of man. It has discovered the "land of absences", the inner midnight ocean which man tries to explore with the help of a small electric torch. It is an attempt at rebellion against the mechanisation of man, against the orderly power of reason, against overlying purposes and motives, against the transformation of man into a perfectly functioning machine. It is a break-out from the life-sentence of daily routine.

The ideal is "liberated man". The Surrealists defend with all the means at their disposal the primary freedom of man, which consists in a free choice between good and evil, between order and chaos, as well as in the liberty to reject a compulsory paradise. This was admitted even by their critics. "All that still moves me is contained in the single word freedom", says Breton. He aims at the wonderful. "The wonderful — only source of the eternal communication between men." (Breton.)

Surrealism is contradiction become corporeal and incarnate. On the Surrealist stage the law of gravity is suspended, which normally keeps things in their terrestrial order; things penetrate each other and give birth to new beings no longer "after their kind, whose seed is in themselves upon the earth". The basic foundations of this cosmos are sunk into an ever-changing ground.

This world-in-a-flux is now fixed and held in rigid snap-shots. The gigantic news-reel does not go by, but suddenly *is*.

Painters spend months and years at work, presenting, immortalizing, and listing the stores of their subterranean warehouse. Deliberately they adopt the meticulous technique of the old masters. Like them, they go about their business calmly and circumspectly, ignoring the unrest and nervousness among their contemporaries, and allowing their thoughts slowly to petrify.

After long exertions, after a process lasting many months, in which the lava of the soul is cooling down, an experience, once liquid, and lasting only a few seconds though often spread over a long time, is at last microscopically nailed down and fixed. Unexpectedly these painters show themselves to be mainly graphic artists. Their fine brush tells a tale, adds one small picture to another, all to be lit up like prints developed by a photographer.

But the spectator, although able to read these hieroglyphics, cannot decipher them. Not unless and until he succeeds in dethroning his controlling reason, and in "breaking the sound barrier of reality in order to enter the realm of fantasy" (L. Zahn), will he be able to do so. When, therefore, people complain that they cannot understand 'modern painting', they are justified, at least as far as Surrealism is concerned. All they can do is to look as receptively as possible and wait for the subconscious to respond to the subconscious of the painter.

LIST OF ILLUSTRATIONS

1. Henri Rousseau. The Sleeping Gipsy. 1897
2. Marc Chagall. A la Russie, aux Anes et aux autres. 1911
3. George Grosz. Heartfield the Engineer
4. Max Ernst. Bird Memorial. 1927
5. Max Ernst. The Woman in the Wall. 1925
6. Max Ernst. The Polish Cavalier. 1934
7. Salvador Dali. The Persistence of Memory. 1931
8. Salvador Dali. The Picture has no Title
9. Yves Tanguy. Scene. 1936
10. Yves Tanguy. Jours de Lenteur. 1947
11. Max Ernst. Night of Love. 1927
12. Max Ernst. The Whole City. 1935
13. Max Ernst. The Nymph Echo. 1946
14. Joan Miró. Still-life with the Old Shoe. 1937
15. René Magritte. The Healer. 1937
16. René Magritte. Daybreak in Cayenne. 1926
17. Paul Delvaux. Pygmalion
18. Maxime van de Woestijne. Self Portrait. 1951
19. Raoul Michau. The Battle of the Potatoes. 1948
20. Wolfgang Hutter. Two Heads. 1954
21. Anton Lehmden. Two Heads. 1953
22. Greta Freist. The Pigeon. 1939
23. Rudolf Hausner. Penelope. 1951
24. Wolfgang Paalen. Cosmogony. 1952

Plate 1

Henri Rousseau (Le Douanier) (born 1844 at Laval, died 1910)

THE SLEEPING GIPSY

Oil, painted 1897

Museum of Modern Art, New York

Rousseau was a friend of Picasso's and the Cubists, a customs official, a Sunday painter, and a man of naïve disposition. But the naïveté of his pictures is matched by a painting technique of extraordinary refinement. This artist of genius, who died in 1910, was no Surrealist. He was, however, a forerunner of Surrealism, since his simple and unsophisticated mind arrived at the same results as did the complicated and ingenious Surrealists. His pictures show the imaginary world of dreams at which Surrealism aims. It may even be said that in his art Surrealism, in the sphere of painting, was fully anticipated and pre-established. Apart from the Douanier, only Max Ernst among Surrealist painters can be said to have entered new territories of creative expression.

Plate 2

Marc Chagall (born 1887 at Vitebsk, Russia)

A LA RUSSIE, AUX ÂNES ET AUX AUTRES

Oil, painted 1911

Musée National d'Art Moderne, Paris

Chagall does not belong to the Surrealists, but represents an original variant of fantastic painting, nourished by impressions of his native Russia and by the mysticism of Chassidic prayer. This is partly expressed in his title: "To Russia, to the Asses and to the Others". Under Cubist influence he arrived at his style of "anecdotal simultané". That is, much may happen simultaneously in his paintings which normally does not happen at all: a dairy maid flies through the air towards a roof where a cow is already being deprived of its milk. A strange spectre causes the girl (literally) to lose her head. These are also dream experiences of a kind, but they differ from Surrealism in that the object is not first surcharged with traumatic meaning and then realistically portrayed, but is made to appear transparent, enthusiastic, and visionary.

Plate 3

George Grosz (born 1893, lives in the U.S.A.)

HEARTFIELD THE ENGINEER

Oil

Museum of Modern Art, New York, A. C. Goodyear Collection

An example of painting from the precincts of Dadaism, the precursor of Surrealism. The few basic elements of this picture are mounted like slogans (Max Ernst frequently used montage). The corner of the room serves at the same time as an axle around which the picture segments rotate cinematographically. There is an analogy to the "cutting" of a film: the statements made in this painting are correlated in similar fashion. Besides, there is irony, as in the contrast of the blank walls of the prison cell with the inscription "Good luck in your new home!" on the flamboyant façade of the period residence, cut into it like a window. The table with prison food is contrasted with the shop-sign "Delicatessen". Similarly, the wheel-work heart of the prisoner — a dismantled alarm clock or gramophone— which he wears as though it were a decoration, recalls the association heart — clock-work, thus indicating the mechanical quality of an engineer's heart. The artistic medium, too, is used ironically, areas being counterpoised against sculptural, photographic details. Cubism had already incorporated in painting various extraneous elements (newspaper cuttings, bits of patterned wallpaper, broken pieces of a mirror) which were in contrast to the otherwise homogeneous medium of paint, and thereby increased tension of form. Here the method is extended in an anecdotal fashion, by formal "underpainting". The picture differs from Surrealist paintings in that it makes definite pointed statements and provokes distinct logical associations. This is in tune with the whole character of the picture, its razor-sharpness and its cutting edges. As on a poster, the oppressed cry out against the power of the state and the authority of the law. Later the Surrealists were to proclaim: throw open the prisons!

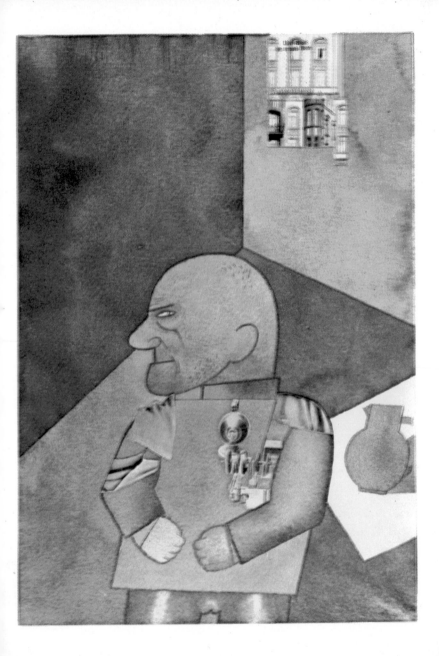

Plate 4

Max Ernst (born 1891 at Brühl, Rhineland)

BIRD MEMORIAL

Oil, painted 1927

Collection Vicomtesse Marie-Laure de Noailles, Paris

In the clear sky floats a group or formation of birds, but different from birds normally floating through the air; strangely stiff and inflated. They are pigeons, but without feathers, perhaps they are even clay pigeons from a shooting range. Or again they may be the creation of an imaginative potter; indeed, they seem to be poised in the ethereal blue in the way a sculpture may be placed against a blank wall in an exhibition or a home. So much for a sober, factual summing-up of what is visible in the picture. Obviously there is much besides, but it refuses to be compressed into a simple formula — this Bird Memorial lit by the evening sun is a secret, complex phenomenon. René Crevel wrote about it:

"Max Ernst, magician of the most delicate vibrations, has released a swarm of pigeons whose warmth, whose fears and whose desires our fingers would like to touch, but are incapable of touching, for bones covered with flesh are not worthy to serve as a perch for birds of the spirit to rest on."

Plate 5

Max Ernst (born 1891 at Brühl, Rhineland)

THE WOMAN IN THE WALL

Oil, painted 1925

Collection Collinet, Paris

A most peculiar painting, hard to read. It appears to face us like the image of a perished civilization whose mythological records have been lost. Perhaps it does not want to be read rationally, but to impress itself upon another level of consciousness. Between two walls which pull apart or draw together, but which at any rate differ distinctly from each other, there appears or vanishes a figure which in parts evokes associations with a female shape. It appears to be of plaster, an ornament stencilled on the wall like the patterns of old-fashioned decorators, or part of the wainscoting. The face is a plumb-line. One may think of the "Metamorphoses", of a "Daphne-of-the-Wall", a personification of the wall, of ancient goddesses with mural crowns. Or, less profoundly, of "The Ghost goes West", where the spectre of the castle is obliged to take part in the piecemeal dismantling of the old building and to move with it across the ocean.

Plate 6

Max Ernst (born 1891 at Brühl, Rhineland)

THE POLISH CAVALIER

Oil, painted 1934

Collection Lazard, Paris

Certain youthful experiences caused Max Ernst to clash with so-called reality. After a short period of science study, he devoted himself entirely to painting and until the First World War was to be found in the slipstream of the Expressionists. After the war he returned to life, in his own words "as a young man who wanted to become a magician and to discover the myth of his time". A Dadaist, he first exhibited in Paris in 1920. Rapidly he acquired an international reputation; there were exhibitions of his work in Brussels, London, Madrid, New York, and Berlin. In 1941 the Rhinelander turned Parisian — one of those most hated by the Nazis — fled to the United States, where in common with Breton, Duchamp, Matta and Tanguy he founded a cosmopolitan branch of Surrealism. Since 1946 he has lived in Arizona. His creative periods are closely related to external events. Next to Picasso's, the world he has created is the richest in modern art. "The Polish Cavalier" is a projection of heraldic emblems onto a landscape in ferment.

CAVALIER
POLONAIS

Plate 7

Salvador Dali (born 1904)

THE PERSISTENCE OF MEMORY

Oil, painted 1931

Museum of Modern Art, New York

What is so hard or even impossible to define in this painting is the strange formation in the centre on which the softened watch rests like a saddle. It is open to interpretation whether this is a living being with worn-off legs, or a skin, or something resembling a face. As a gesture or attitude, however, the thing can be defined clearly: it is something defeated, exhausted, limp and flaccid, something which could move no further and was stranded on the rocks. The three watches bear a similar expression of stretchiness and glue-like fluidity. This doughy quality is contrasted with the metallic hardness of the fourth watch, the barrenness of the tree, the ruggedness of the rocky coastline. Absolute quiet reigns. Light and shade seem to creep on slowly. If anything moves in this clear glassy painting, it does so lazily, viscously, trailingly. The block and the rigid tree trunk on the left are resisting the forward movement on the right. The effect of sluggish inertia is heightened at the same time by the swarms of busily crawling ants eating away at honey-like dripping time. On the whole, something firm and immobile is set against anything which runs, creeps, stretches and flows — all, without exception, words indicating the passage of time — while all the time-pieces are shown in a drippy condition. Here we are confronted with personal time as distinct from measurable time, for everyone to stretch according to his own wishes. Remembrance, too, which we drag about with us, belongs to a realm where clock time is not valid.

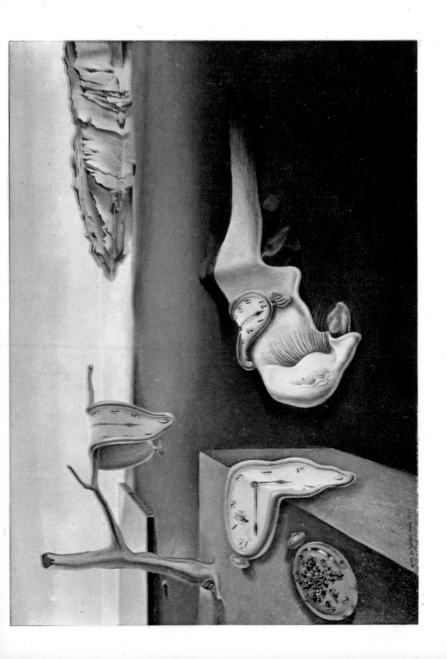

Plate 8

Salvador Dali (born 1904)

THE PICTURE HAS NO TITLE

Collection Filipacchi, Paris

The first impression is: here is someone in flight, wanting to hide, wanting to turn into, and fuse with, the rock. The structure of the picture rests upon two dividing lines, both running obliquely towards the frame: on the left the tilted vertical of the figure and, somewhat aslant against the horizon, the edge of the shadow. The entire dark area in between seems to follow this movement of an escape from the world. An escape from the void, a plunge into the rock through the gate of shadow. The rock shows a cleavage where it may be entered. The body gleams faintly, on the shoulders glitter a few shells, the head has already turned into brightly lit stones, phosphorescing as though in decay. The ornament in the side of the rock is the secret formula of metamorphosis.

Plate 9

Yves Tanguy (born 1900, died 1955)

SCÈNE

Oil painted 1936

Private collection, Paris

Yves Tanguy was born in Paris of Breton parents, started life at sea and was induced to paint by a picture of Giorgio de Chirico's. From 1925 onward he belonged to the Surrealist group in Paris. In 1939 he emigrated to the United States and in 1948 became an American citizen. He died in January 1955 at Woodbury, Connecticut. It can be said that even as a painter he remained a seaman. His paintings are invariably related to the sea: the bizarre wreckage of his shapes suggests fantastically rigged boats; salt water seems to have washed from his canvas all reflective, sentimental associations; the melancholy of endless horizons has been banished from his pictures.

Plate 10

Yves Tanguy (born 1900, died 1955)

JOURS DE LENTEUR

Oil, painted 1947

Musée National d'Art Moderne, Paris

This painting is typical of Tanguy's manner in which Surrealism and non-representational art are fused. There are indeed objects represented in it, but it would be impossible to name them, even though they suggest shells and other things washed up on the beach; bits of wood or pebbles polished by the sea; then again they recall sculptures by Henry Moore. All these tidal associations are called up by the background and underground, or rather by the plain with its shadowy horizon resembling a sea shore or desert sands. The objects are conceived as gliding, and seem to float like seaweed or jelly-fish; but they float in the air; they are solid and capable of casting deep shadows. These things are really gestures, they are objects rising, spreading out, sitting enthroned or tap-dancing, objects performing a little scene. The sandy plain here stands for the landscape of the unconscious, the dream-like, the unreal, and the flotsam and jetsam calmly expresses what cannot be grasped by our conscious mind.

Plâte 11

Max Ernst (born 1891 at Brühl, Rhineland)

NIGHT OF LOVE

Painted 1927

Pierre Matisse Gallery, New York

A nocturnal picture. A winding and weaving of half-recognizable figures stretching, embracing, stepping apart against the background of a strange slanting area, is suddenly surprised by a beam of light. The light is harsh, and it lifts particles of the figures off the ground with which they form a unity of colour. The result is a feeling of embarrassment and repression.

This painting is a dream which has oppressed us and whose images and figures evade us at the moment of waking, a dream which escapes among the first returning sparks of consciousness. A harsh beam of light suddenly bursting in on a dream — that is the experience transmitted by this picture. It wishes to explain nothing, it only wants to transfix what it sees; it is a flashbulb snapshot of a psychological occurence.

Dreams are an important field for Surrealist research. Here Max Ernst was able considerably to widen our range of vision, not by depicting his own dreams, but by recording what he saw and experienced on the borderline between outer and inner world.

Plate 12

Max Ernst (born 1891 at Brühl, Rhineland)

THE WHOLE CITY

Oil, painted 1935

Edouard Loeb Gallery, Paris*

Shapes are here superimposed upon each other like a heap of punched metal strips, technical waste matter. The Dadaists were the first to use "banal" means. Kurt Schwitters glued his pictures together from railway tickets and similar things gathered up at random. Why not? Why should oil paint be considered nobler matter? The essential point is that the material used should be transformed into a creation of shape and tension. In this painting, too, oil paint which looks as though it had been stencilled onto the canvas with the help of metal strips is transformed into something else, no longer indicative of its material origin: the triumph of the spirit over matter. Academic accomplishment which every copyist can master is here belittled; imagination takes its place. The punched metal strips turn into a prehistoric terrace landscape, into dead cities with a forbidding stare, thistles growing outside their walls.

* THE CITADEL, another version of this picture, now hangs in the Tate Gallery.

Plate 13

Max Ernst (born 1891 at Brühl, Rhineland)

THE NYMPH ECHO

Oil, painted 1946

Private collection, Paris

Not a very amiable being, this nymph! It may have sprung from the mythology of some primeval epoch of the earth, or it may be the spectre of the jungle, the carnivorous hobgoblin of a plant, or the first of all hamadryads, those sprites of the trees. It is certainly more dangerous than the nymphs and nereids of Arnold Boecklin who go about their business in a happy-go-lucky fashion. This one with its vampire-snout, lurking like a chlorophyll spider, but endowed with the limbs of a praying mantis, under the vicious beauty of the tufts of flowers, is a more gruesome personification of wilderness than are the graceful nymphs whom the god Pan led in their nocturnal dance.

Plate 14

Joan Miró (born 1893 at Montroig, Barcelona)

STILL-LIFE WITH THE OLD SHOE

Painted 1937

James Thrall Soby Collection, Farmington, U.S.A.

The first impression of this painting is of a chopping and changing, a constant reversion of various forms. Much remains uncertain even after closer scrutiny, although some of the shapes are sharply outlined. The objects in this still-life, among which the shoe on the right springs first into view, put in momentary appearances as though under a vacillating light. Hence the stormy, sultry, uncanny, and threatening atmosphere of the whole picture.

There is no clear and unequivocal relation between the objects. The shoe is too big for the loaf behind it. A hand with six fingers is stuck into fruit as with the prongs of a fork. The centre axle consists of a thing dented completely out of shape and beyond recognition, a burst and rust-eaten thermos flask perhaps, around which the rest have collected as on a rubbish-heap — objects from one of the Andersen fairy tales about plain, homely, cast-off things ("The Bottle-neck", "The Mending Needle", "The Collar"). This is a nightmare of a tramp. These shabby objects, polished by use, are lent a look of significance by the peculiar lighting. The shoe could be projected onto a glass plate; it is surrounded by an aura. The thermos flask looks as though lit up from the inside. Their phosphorescence makes these rotting objects appear precious like a treasure of glowing jewels. There is sheet-lightning along the horizon, and the air is filled with violently rising shadows cast by objects onto what appear to be walls of mist. The whole recalls the sudden and magical illumination of cosmic stage-props.

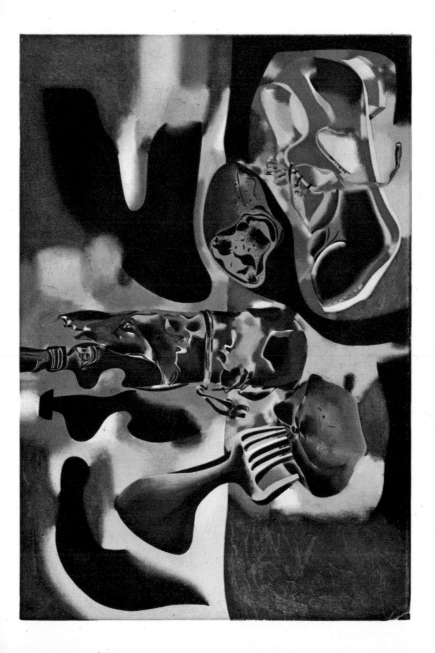

Plate 15

René Magritte (born 1898)

THE HEALER

Oil, painted 1937

Collection J. B. Urvater, Brussels

Magritte calls the old man, who takes up the entire width of his painting, a healer. With walking-stick and satchel he has sat down to rest by the seashore. He is no eminent physician, rather a wandering country doctor or private male nurse. His cloak or "robe" has slipped open to reveal his inner self. In the place of a head and body with a heart and other organs, Magritte, with dry humour, reveals a cage wherein the old man keeps a pair of white and peaceable birds, one of which cautiously ventures into the open.

Plate 16

René Magritte (born 1898)

DAYBREAK IN CAYENNE

Oil, painted 1926

Collection J. B. Urvater, Brussels

Magritte dispenses with refinement. Whenever he ponders, he resembles an unsophisticated Sunday painter. Inspiration for his paintings comes from popular notions and emotions; he takes pleasure in the side-shows at a fair, the naive faith of small votive pictures in holy shrines. His symbols have the character of wood-cuts. Like Léger he isolates objects (see the volume "Cubism" in this series, plate 18), and thus has certain affinities with the Cubist painter. But Léger's objects are entirely real, they are "objectively" there, placed in a room without perspective, while Magritte's objects, such as his folded hands, his burning candle, the branches in the sky, are all seen in a symbolist perspective and directed towards something. It is all in tune with miraculous deliverance and wayside votive offerings. In this painting Magritte seems to symbolise the damnation of a penal settlement, the thorny path of everyday routine beginning at each sunrise, the spider in the flesh of hopelessness, the dawn of the damned and oppressed for whom there is no salvation.

Plate 17

Paul Delvaux (born 1897)

PYGMALION

Oil

Collection Mme Purna, Palais des Beaux Arts, Brussels

This reproduction is only a section of a larger painting (its right half). The cracks in the ground and the pavement indicate the hidden dual character of our existence. Two spheres of experience penetrate each other, the realm of dream and the realm of wakefulness, of wonder and of everyday life. The man with the hat blindly passes the extraordinary vision, she on her part is insensitive to the trivial atmosphere of a seaside town out of season. But wherever two spheres of experience interweave, the atmosphere grows strangely tight, movements are made as though under pressure, sparks crackle around the inductors, pebbles blow up, sudden transformations occur.

Plate 18

Maxime van de Woestijne (born 1911)

SELF PORTRAIT

Oil, painted 1951

Collection J. B. Urvater, Brussels

The dream experiences of Woestijne, as depicted in this "Face", differ distinctly
from the Surrealism of other Belgian painters like Magritte and Delvaux. This
portrayal of an artist's identity has become all painter's eye, all dream vision.
The artist portrays himself from the inside looking outwards, from deep inside
a towering enclosure where the observing eye breaks out from a crate. The
limitations of inner space are suspended, as are the dead weight and proportion
of things in relation to each other; one travels through gigantic and monstrous
space which, echoing with emptiness, is at the same time near and far; closed up
yet leaving open a mousehole whence to escape; the floor is an immense mirror.
Here man is imprisoned, flies in the air, and yet burdens others — for the crate
is merely a synonym for "burden". Hair fumes from the crate and forms a figure.
The general mood is one of instability.

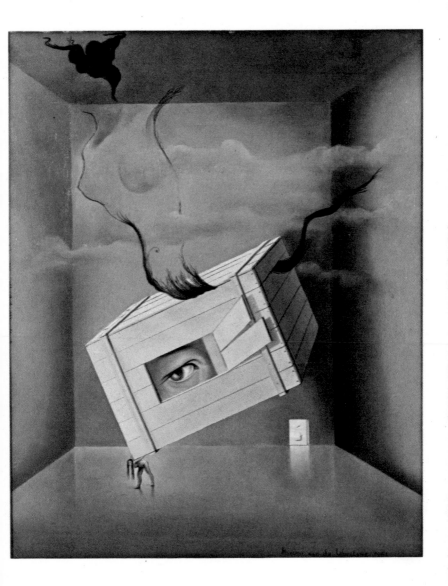

Plate 19

Raoul Michau

THE BATTLE OF THE POTATOES

Painted 1948

Musée National d'Art Moderne, Paris

An easily understood allegory: Potatoes armed with pikes and bars are forming a phalanx and waging a peasant's war under a sultry sky. Battle pictures from Altdorfer down to the 19th century shine through. Not unhumorously, the rustling of banners is divested of heroic meaning. It is significant that the arms carried by these potato troops are their own shoots sprouting in the dark of the cellar, on that underground level to which the Surrealists like to descend.

Plate 20

Wolfgang Hutter (born 1928 in Vienna)

TWO HEADS

Watercolour, painted 1954

Property of the artist

The first and obvious thing about this painting is its preciousness. Two figures and between them a plant figuring in no botanical text-book, are arranged symmetrically, almost like a playing card. As in the imaginative ornamental friezes of the 16th century, or of Lukas Kilian, where human figures are intertwined with trellis-work, man here is strangely transfixed. The young man gazes intently at the woman without actually looking at her. There is a great silence around the two heads, but above them where blossoms and leaves advance into space like bunting, all is in airy movement. The two could be smoking a water-pipe, they may both be blowing up a flower calix or else the calix is growing from their mouths — at all events, the plant is meant to unite them ceremoniously, and at the same time to separate them. It is a kind of fantastic flower of life through which they communicate.

With Ernst Fuchs, Rudolf Hausner, Fritz Janschka, and Anton Lehmden, W. Hutter belongs to a group of young painters who, after the Second World War, carried on the Surrealist tradition and attracted attention in Vienna, no less by their original choice of subject than by the complete mastery of their craft. Hutter's figures are always like exotic, half-real flowers, and his landscapes are an artificial paradise.

Plate 21

Anton Lehmden (born 1929 at Neutra)

TWO HEADS

Watercolour, painted 1953

Property of the artist

Lehmden has painted a series of most impressive war paintings, deserted battle-fields, no-man's-land, clashes of armoured vehicles, and men tearing each other to pieces. Once again war is responsible for the subject chosen by this Surrealist painter. Lehmden's paintings are a denunciation of war in which his feeling for nature plays an important part. In his spacious landscapes in the style of the "Danubean school", but cleared of all shagginess, man appears as a lonely being, cast out like a gipsy, and seeking refuge with others. By pure coincidence, three painters have been included in this volume (Hutter, Lehmden and Hausner) who are attracted by the same basic theme.

Plate 22
Greta Freist (born in Vienna, lives in Paris)

THE PIGEON

Oil, painted 1939

Property of the artist

A painting from the late period of Surrealism proper. The physical condition of fantasy here depicted seems to connect it, across a wide span, with still-lifes of the 16th to the 19th centuries. The way in which objects luxuriantly overgrow each other, disorderly as in landscape, may be called allegorical, but it could certainly be interpreted by psycho-analytical methods. The gorge, the vista, the vegetation, the bizarre rock, the root-like rope, the serpent — all these belong to a magic experience of the objective world (no less than de Chirico's furniture mentioned in the introduction), the reptile enclosure in its autumnal mood is irrational space. Here nature is not seen in terms of the idyllic, heroic, or sentimental, nor as a prospect, a paradise, "humanized", but as desert nature, small, near, not unduly wild, where living beings are alien to each other. It is a largely non-human interpretation of nature.

Plate 23

Rudolf Hausner (born 1914 in Vienna)

PENELOPE

Watercolour, painted 1951

Property of the artist

It is the deliberate intention of the younger generation of Surrealists to concern themselves with the subject of communication. This is seen by Hutter as a "miracle of conjunction", by Lehmden as "refuge" — and Rudolf Hausner in his "Penelope" chooses to play on the old theme of "separation". Hausner spent several years painting a single picture of medium size (which earned him some ridicule), working over section after section with an ever-increasing refinement of observation. As a result, there are today not many such masters of realistic treatment. The painting referred to was called "Ulysses"; his watercolour "Penelope" is therefore a companion piece to the larger picture.

The younger generation of Surrealists, especially in Austria, while making more sparing use of traditional key situations and achieving their own allegorical means of expression, seem to prefer the personal sphere to the microcosm and macrocosm of the objective world. There are no more expeditions and raids across the desert, the jungle, dead cities, and geological periods. The objects of dream experience remain subordinated to man, as in Hausner's painting where a woman most gracefully presents a few domestic objects on a fragile tray; a small, unstable family of things. While man crashes to the ground outside, woman upholds and supports the family. The silence is rent by catastrophe; as often in Hausner's pictures, space is overturned. The red ball signifies the perfect creation, happiness, the sun, light, fruit, and joy.

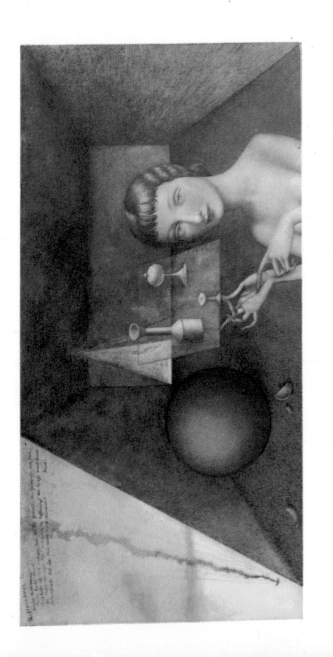

Plate 24

Wolfgang Paalen

COSMOGONY

Oil, painted 1952

Collection Madeleine Rousseau, Paris

Strictly speaking, Wolfgang Paalen's picture no longer belongs to Surrealism. It is an off-shoot tending towards abstract painting. This kinship results from the fantastic, miraculous character of the shining vision whose exotic plumage is interwoven with Byzantine colouring.

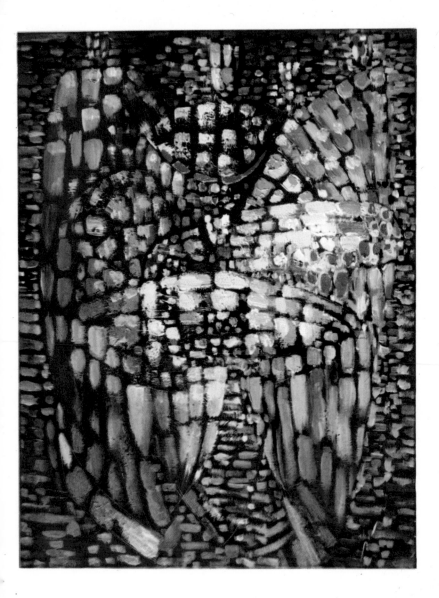